HIDDEN FIGURES

Margot Lee Shetterly

Adapted by Jane Rollason

LEVEL 3

SCHOLASTIC

Adapted by: Jane Rollason

Publisher: Gordon Knowles

Editor: Fiona Davis

Designer: Dawn Wilson

Picture research: Pupak Navabpour

Photo credits:
Cover: "HIDDEN FIGURES" Cover art © 2019 Twentieth Century Fox Film Corporation.
All Rights Reserved.

Pages 4 & 5: SmithCollection/Gabo/Getty Images; 20th Century Fox/Allstar, Courtesy of 20th Century Fox; NASA;
pop_jop/iStockphoto.
Pages 9–11: Science History Images/Alamy; Bettmann/Getty Images.
Page 13: The Life Picture Collection, Photo Quest/Getty Images.
Pages 16–20: Underwood Archives/Getty Images; B. Christopher, PF aircraft/Alamy;
Dr G. Settles/Science Photo Library.
Pages 23–25: Universal Images Group, US Navy/Getty Images.
Pages 27–30: Universal Images Group/Getty Images; AP Footage/Alamy.
Page 35: B. Nye/NASA.
Pages 38–41: Bettmann, Ullstein Bild/Getty Images; NASA.
Page 45: NASA/Eyevine.
Pages 49–51: NASA; The Life Picture Collection/Getty Images
Pages 53–56: Paramount/Allstar; C. Clarivan/Science Photo Library; NASA.
Pages 58 & 59: gmutlu, orplayday/iStockphoto; NASA.

First published in Great Britain by William Collins in 2016
First published in the United States by William Morrow, an imprint of HarperCollinsPublishers in 2016

This William Collins paperback edition published 2017

1

Published by Scholastic Ltd. 2020

Mary Glasgow Magazines (Scholastic Ltd.)
Euston House
24 Eversholt Street
London NW1 IDB

Printed in Malaysia

Contents

HIDDEN FIGURES

Dorothy Vaughan got a maths degree in 1929 and became a high school maths teacher in Farmville, Virginia.

DOROTHY VAUGHAN

Mary Jackson grew up in Hampton, Virginia, and studied maths and physics at Hampton University in the early 1940s.

Katherine Johnson was born in 1918, and her skill with figures was clear when she was a child. By the time she was eighteen, she had completed a degree in maths.

PLACES

US research into flight and spacecraft design began at the NACA in Virginia on the east coast in 1915.

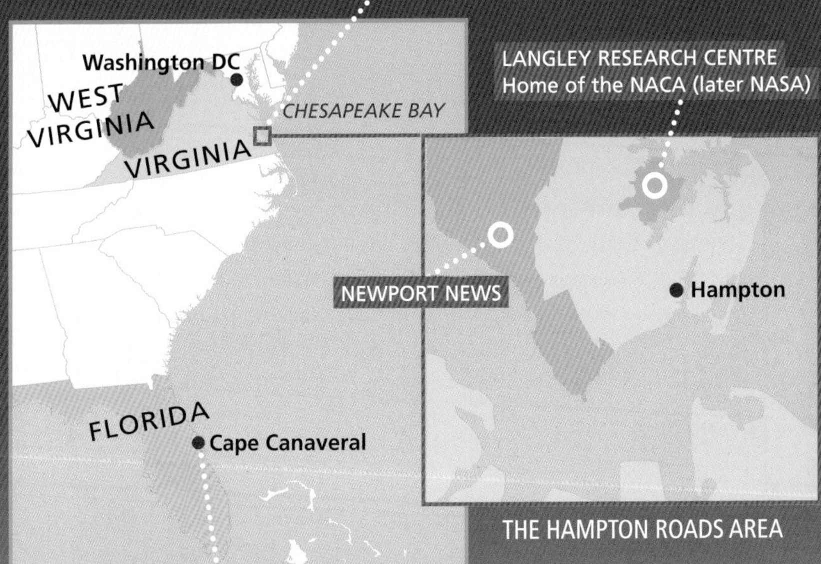

The first US spacecraft were launched from Cape Canaveral in Florida.

TIMELINE OF **HIDDEN FIGURES**

1929 Wall Street Crash
Millions of people lost everything after money markets in the US crashed.

1929–1939 Great Depression
After the Wall Street Crash, many businesses and shops closed. Millions of people lost their jobs, not just in the US but around the world.

1939–1945 In **World War II** the United States and the Soviet Union fought on the same side – against Germany and Japan.

1941 Japan bombed **Pearl Harbor** in Hawaii, in the United States, and the US immediately joined the war.

8th May 1945 VE Day
Victory in Europe Day ended the war in Europe.

August 1945 The United States dropped the world's first **atomic bombs** on Hiroshima and Nagasaki in Japan to end World War II.

15th August 1945 VJ Day
Victory over Japan Day ended the war in Asia.

1947–1991 Cold War
After the end of World War II, the world had two superpowers. The United States led Western countries, calling themselves 'the free world'. Eastern European countries were controlled by the Communist Soviet Union. The Cold War was mostly a war of ideas. Both superpowers wanted the newly independent countries in Asia, Africa and the Caribbean to follow their ideas. The Cold War ended with the fall of the Soviet Union in 1991.

1949 The Soviet Union tested their first **atomic bomb**.

1950–1953 Korean War

North Korean soldiers crossed into South Korea, and war began. The Soviet Union helped the North. The United States sent soldiers and guns to the South.

September 1957 Little Rock Nine

Nine black students began school at the all-white Central High School in Little Rock, Arkansas. The Governor of Arkansas tried to stop them. The President of the US sent in soldiers to take them into school.

October 1957 Sputnik 1

The Soviet Union successfully sent the first ever **satellite** into orbit around the earth.

1958–1963 Project Mercury

The first US **spaceflight** programme.

28th August 1963 The March on Washington

Martin Luther King spoke to a quarter of a million people. 'I have a dream,' he famously told them.

1965 The last of the **Jim Crow laws** came to an end. Following the end of slavery in the US in 1865, the Southern states of the US had brought in their own laws to segregate the white and black communities.

27th January 1967 Apollo 1 space mission ended in disaster.

4th April 1968 Martin Luther King was shot dead.

20th July 1969 The US **Apollo 11** space mission put the first **man on the moon**.

HIDDEN FIGURES

CHAPTER 1

A door opens

It was nearly 40°C and extremely uncomfortable. Dorothy Vaughan was sorting socks in a room full of washing machines at Camp Pickett, Virginia. The socks belonged to American soldiers who were training at Camp Pickett before going to war.

All the women around her were black. Most of them had worked in the cigarette factories before the war. Not Dorothy. She was a maths teacher and had been to college. This was her second job, bringing in extra dollars in the school holidays. Washerwomen were the lowest paid of all war workers, but Dorothy still earned more sorting socks than teaching. She needed the money for her family of four young children. Dorothy didn't think she was too good to wash socks. She saw no difference between herself and the other workers. She wanted to send her children to college and each cent she earned would help to pay for it.

As well as being brilliant at maths, Dorothy had been a perfect student. At the age of only fifteen, she had won a place to study maths at Wilberforce University in Ohio. She was then offered a place at Howard University in Washington DC, the top university for black students. It was bad timing for Dorothy, however, as it was 1929, the year of the Wall Street Crash. The Great Depression followed, and jobs were lost everywhere as factories and shops closed. Dorothy's parents needed help to pay the family's bills and to send Dorothy's sister to college.

Instead of studying for a higher maths degree at Howard, Dorothy trained to be a teacher.

A teaching job came up at a school in Farmville, Virginia, and Dorothy moved there. She soon met Howard Vaughan, tall and handsome, and they married that same year. Working as a doorman in expensive hotels, Howard travelled from city to city with the tourist seasons. Dorothy stayed in Farmville, where Howard's parents owned a large house with plenty of space for the young family. Dorothy never had a free moment, and she never turned down a chance to put money in the bank. Even on Sundays, she earned money by playing the piano at a local church.

Over 150 kilometres from Farmville, in the Hampton Roads area of Virginia, was a place called Langley.

Langley Research Centre wind tunnel, 1934

Langley was the home of the NACA*, where US aircraft were designed. On the beautiful Chesapeake Bay were buildings full of planes and huge wind tunnels for testing them. The United States had joined World War ll in 1941 and all the buildings were painted dark green to hide them from enemy spy planes.

American President Franklin D. Roosevelt realised that air power would be the key to winning World War II. Unlike in World War I, planes were now able to carry soldiers, guns and, most importantly, bombs. In 1938, the US was making a thousand planes a year. In 1941, President Roosevelt ordered the country to make 50,000 planes a year. In fact, by 1943, the US was producing 75,000 planes a year, far more than the enemy countries of Germany and Japan.

Designing and testing planes needed millions of calculations. Physics kept planes in the air, and physics meant maths. Langley needed mathematicians. New employees could be men or women, black or white, but they had to be excellent at maths.

Although it was nearly one hundred years since the end of slavery, black Americans were a long way from equality with white Americans. In Southern states like Virginia, whites and blacks were segregated in all areas of life. White people didn't share schools, restaurants, toilets, buses or even drinking water with black people. Workplaces were segregated too. But with the war on, black workers were in a strong position. 'Give us well-paid war jobs too,' they said to the government. President Roosevelt knew they were right. In 1941, he signed a new law. From then on, all jobs were open to everyone.

* National Advisory Committee for Aeronautics

Oklahoma City, 1939

Langley wanted to employ black women as computers*. But Langley was in the state of Virginia where, even after 1941, black and white people were not allowed to live or work together. Langley's answer was an office away from the other buildings. It was called the West Area, and in 1943, the first female black mathematicians arrived. A new sign went up over the door to the West Area toilet. It said 'Coloured Girls'**.

On her way home from washing socks in Camp Pickett, Dorothy always checked the job notices in the post office. One spring day in 1943, a notice caught her eye. The NACA needed mathematicians. Dorothy had read stories in the black newspapers about good jobs for women and good jobs for black women. A job as a mathematician! Dorothy picked up a form and took it home.

* Before there were electronic computers, maths was done by human 'computers'. The mathematicians in this story are called 'computers'.
** The word 'Coloured' is not used today, but was widely used at the time when this story takes place.

CHAPTER 2
The Coloured line

'I'll be back for Christmas,' said Dorothy, and climbed into the taxi. Her husband, her four children and their grandparents stood in front of their big house and waved. Dorothy was leaving behind twelve years of maths teaching and home building in Farmville. She was starting on a 225-kilometre journey to a new life.

The job offer had come: *Mathematician, grade 1, $2,000 per year until the end of the war, and a further six months after that date.* Working at Langley meant a six-day week in an office too far away from Farmville for weekend visits. With their family and community around them, Dorothy knew that her children's busy lives would hardly change. They were used to their mother's long working days and their father being away from home for months at a time. 'I'll miss them more than they'll miss me,' she thought, as she sat in the Coloured waiting room at the bus station.

Stepping off the bus into Newport News was like entering another country. The town was beside the James River, where warships were lined up ready to sail across the oceans. Thousands of workers climbed all over them, preparing them to fight. Military vehicles drove onto them. There were soldiers and sailors of all ages and races, both men and women. As well as the noise from the ships, there was building work everywhere. There were smells from restaurants, vehicles, smoke and the sea. People waited in lines to buy sugar, coffee, butter and meat. The buses were crowded. Cinemas were open all day, banks were open all night, and the hospitals and schools were full. The war machine never stopped.

THE JIM CROW LAWS

Florida, USA

The Jim Crow laws in Virginia and other Southern states dated back to the 1870s. Slavery might be over, but many whites in the South still believed that whites were better than blacks. Everything was segregated: housing, schools, shops, restaurants, hospitals, banks, trains and buses.

Each city bus had a Coloured line. There was a door for whites at the front of the bus and a door for blacks at the back. White people sat in the front half, black people were at the back behind the 'Coloured line'. If a black person sat in a 'white' seat, they had to pay a fine. Or worse, the police pulled them off the bus and took them to the police station.

North Carolina, USA, 1940

Newport News was one of several small towns around Chesapeake Bay, on the coast of Virginia. The area was called Hampton Roads. Once home to farms, fishing communities and forests, the main business of Hampton Roads was now war. It was a powerful military capital.

Prices for rooms and flats had doubled, but there was still a waiting list because there weren't enough homes for the war workers. The government built two new towns within the city. Newsome Park had 1,200 homes for blacks. Copeland Park had 4,000 homes for whites.

Dorothy carried her small suitcase to her single room in her new home. For five dollars a week, she got a bed and two meals a day in a house in Newsome Park. It was a nice area with good houses, local shops and a shiny new hospital. Dorothy had three days to get to know her new world before she had to report to Langley for work.

When the US entered World War II, President Roosevelt had made a promise to protect the right of all people to be free. He was talking about the Jews in Nazi Germany, but things were not much better for the black people in the Southern states of his own country. One black newspaper wrote, 'Help us to get rights here at home first before you tell us to free other peoples and go and die in a foreign land.'

The black newspapers played an important part in joining black groups and actions together across the country. The fight for rights was beginning to come together in one movement, called the Civil Rights movement. 'Let black American soldiers use the double VV for a double victory,' said one newspaper, the *Pittsburgh Courier*. 'The first V is for victory over the enemy abroad, the second V is for victory over racism at home.'

On 1st December 1943, the leaders of the US, Britain and the Soviet Union met to plan D-Day. They were going to land their soldiers on the coast of France and begin the ground attack on Germany. In Newport News, Dorothy sat behind the Coloured line on the bus to Langley, on her way to her first day at work.

CHAPTER 3
The question of flight

As the NACA grew more important during the war, more and more buildings were needed. Langley was now so big you had to take a bus from one side to the other. Dorothy's new office was in the West Area, right on the edge, with fields and woods beyond. And high above the office buildings were the huge metal wind tunnels. Visitors said it was like being in a science fiction film.

The West Area Computers Unit wasn't much different from Dorothy's classroom in Farmville. There were desks in lines with an office manager instead of a teacher. Everyone in the room was a computer, and all you could hear was the sound of Friden calculating machines.

Using a Friden calculating machine, 1940s

There were other offices full of computers in the East Area of Langley. The only difference in the West Area office was that the twenty women sitting at the desks were black. In 1940, just two percent of black women had college degrees, compared to ten percent of white women and thirty-three percent of white men. Sixty percent of black females with degrees became school teachers, but zero percent became engineers. So working at the biggest and best aeronautical centre in the world was a special achievement.

Often black workers felt they had to be twice as good as white people to achieve half as much. They made sure they were always on time, always worked hard, never made mistakes, dressed well and were polite. The West Area computers always wanted to show that they were equal or better.

The government wanted the NACA to make military aircraft as powerful, safe and fast as possible. Their work was central to winning the war. On a visit to Langley in November 1943, the Secretary of the Navy, Frank Knox, spoke to the NACA workers. 'You men and women working here far from the sound of drums and guns,' he said, 'are winning your part of this war.'

The crowd of 1,500 NACA workers listening to Knox were mainly white men. In one corner was a group of black men in workmen's jeans, not shirts and ties. There were only a few white women in the crowd and even fewer black women. After Secretary Knox had spoken, the black women walked to the cafeteria. Everyone used the same cafeteria, and people usually chose to sit in the same groups. But the black women had no choice. A handwritten sign on a table at the back said 'Coloured computers', so the black women sat there. It was the only sign in the room.

The sign wasn't unusual. But because people were employed at Langley for their maths skills, it seemed especially unnecessary. The women pushed the sign away while they were eating, pretending it wasn't there. In the office, the women felt equal. But when they went to the cafeteria or the toilets, the signs made it clear that not everyone felt that way.

One West Area computer, Miriam Mann, finally decided it was too much. Miriam was not very tall, but she had a big personality. She simply put the sign in her handbag. Her friends laughed, but they were worried for Miriam. After a week, a new sign appeared. It quickly disappeared into Miriam's bag again.

'You're going to lose your job over that sign, Miriam,' said her husband.

'Fine,' said Miriam. 'I'll just have to find another job.'

Before the war was over, Miriam put the sign into her handbag for the last time. No new sign appeared. It was one small victory on the road to equality.

Local Hampton people had little idea what happened at Langley. In the town they saw the engineers and scientists, many of whom came from California, New York or even Europe. They didn't wear ties and they looked as if they had slept in their shirts. They read books while they were driving their cars to work. The sales people in local garages and electrical shops would hide when someone from the NACA came in because they asked impossible questions about how a new car or a new television worked. Locals simply called them the 'NACA nuts'*.

On top of their six-day week, Dorothy and other new girls took a course in aerodynamics twice a week after work, plus a two-hour lesson in a wind tunnel and four hours' homework. Their teachers were some of the best physicists in town.

* A 'nut' is someone who is a big fan of something.

AERODYNAMICS: HOW DOES A PLANE FLY?

There are four forces of flight: weight, lift, drag and thrust. These forces control how a plane moves up or down and how fast or slow it travels.

WEIGHT is the force which comes from gravity pulling an object to the ground. Power is needed to push a plane into the air. The heavier the plane, the more power is needed.

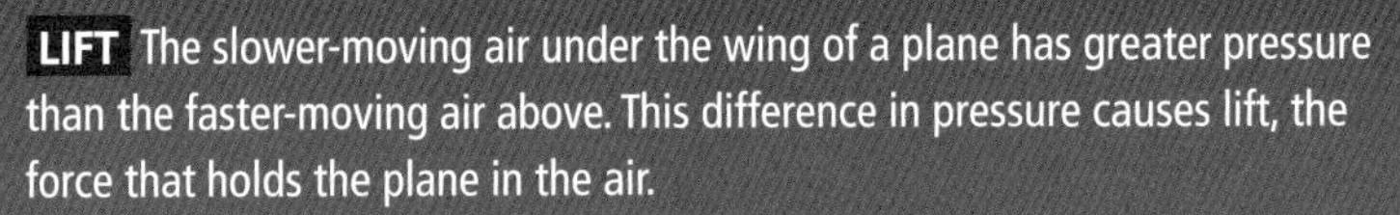

LIFT The slower-moving air under the wing of a plane has greater pressure than the faster-moving air above. This difference in pressure causes lift, the force that holds the plane in the air.

DRAG is the force that slows an object down when it is moving. The shape of an object is important – a rounded object has less drag than a flat one.

THRUST is the force that moves an object forwards. It's the opposite of drag. For an aircraft to move forwards, it must have more thrust than drag.

Research in the NACA's wind tunnels produced a new wing shape that gave more lift. The first plane designed to use this shape was the Mustang.

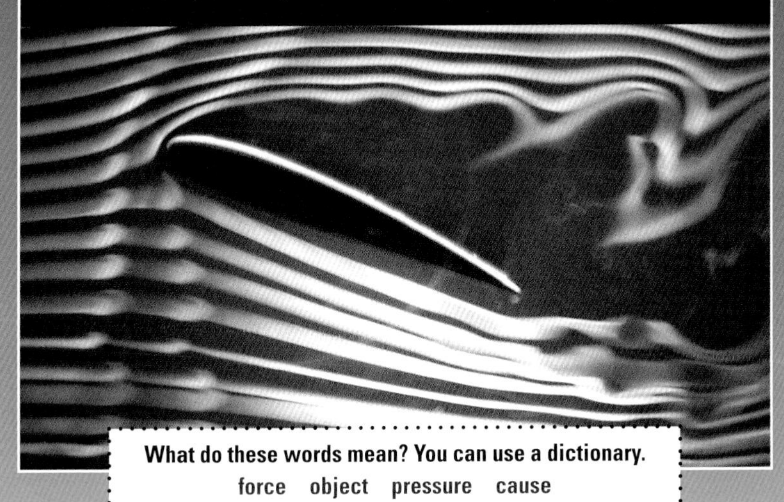

What do these words mean? You can use a dictionary.

force object pressure cause

Dorothy had never been on a plane. But the question of flight now had her full attention. Scientists still had a lot to learn about flight. They had to come up with new ideas, do the maths, try out their ideas and be lucky. In the early days, pilots could only test new ideas by flying. Many died. Now the NACA had wind tunnels, which offered testing without the danger. The wind moving over the plane was similar to the plane moving through the air at speed. Langley built a number of wind tunnels, each testing a different part of flight. One of the tunnels was large enough to hold a full-sized plane.

The wind tunnel was never exactly the same as flying through the air. One of Dorothy's first jobs was to calculate the difference between the two. This was key to the NACA's success. The tunnels ran all night, as the engineers pushed the machines for answers to their questions. Nobody in the world could match the NACA's wind tunnels.

Readers of black newspapers around the country began to follow the exciting adventures of the Tuskegee airmen.

Tuskegee airmen

The Tuskegee airmen were African-American pilots fighting in the skies over Europe. By 1944 they were flying Mustang aircraft, which protected bomber planes on their missions. Flying a Mustang was like riding a top racehorse. The Tuskegee airmen loved it. And down on the ground, working out the maths for those Mustangs, was Dorothy.

The computers often worked on one small part of a bigger problem. They might not hear anything about their work until they read the results in *Air Scoop**. For many engineers, the computers were part of the equipment; they took in one set of figures and gave out another. Once a job was finished, the numbers disappeared into the secret world of the engineers. But Dorothy knew her work was making a difference in the war. As the months passed, Dorothy grew more confident with the ideas, the numbers and the people at Langley, and she too was an NACA nut.

* *Air Scoop* was a newspaper for everyone working at Langley.

CHAPTER 4
VJ Day

Dorothy had a plan. The war didn't take holidays and it was hard for Dorothy to get time to see her children. On a day off she would take the earliest bus to Farmville, returning as late as she could. The numbers on her calculating machine would swim before her tired eyes the following day.

On the Fourth of July holiday in 1944, Dorothy signed up for a two-bedroom house in Newsome Park. When the government built Newport News, they only meant it to last as long as the war. The NACA only meant Dorothy's job to last as long as the war too. But she decided to take a chance, and now she had the keys to a new home. It was so new that the floors were still covered in pink paper. Moving in was like opening a birthday present. She went back to Farmville to get her children.

Dorothy's four children started the new year at Newsome Park School. Her husband, Howard, came when he could. But it was crowded and noisy in the little home, and far from his old mother in Farmville. He never stayed long, and Dorothy sent the children to Farmville for the summer holidays. Although Dorothy and Howard were still married, they didn't live together for the rest of their lives.

Who could ever forget the summer of 1945? It was 7.03 in the evening on 15th August. Everyone came out into the streets. Shopkeepers closed their doors for the day. People cried and laughed, and held hands with strangers. Bands played and children danced around cars. Churches filled and people gave thanks. It was VJ Day, and the war was over!

VJ Day in New York City

The war had been like a train travelling at high speed. Now it had reached its final stop. What next for the passengers? Just three weeks after VJ Day, 1,500 ship workers in Newport News lost their jobs. Two million American women, both black and white, lost their jobs before the end of August. Many of the jobs were given to returning soldiers. For some women, the war had changed the way they saw their lives and they refused to go back to the kitchen and childcare. 'Many husbands will return home to find strong, independent women,' wrote one journalist.

Dorothy was still waiting to hear about the future of her job but she had a feeling she was safe at Langley.

She loved her job and she knew she was good at it. She decided to sign up for two more years in the house. Dorothy's children had become used to their much smaller home and their new way of life. Dorothy had given the second bedroom to a returning soldier and his wife, who looked after the children during the day.

On days off, the children played at a small lake which lay between Newsome Park and the white community of Copeland Park. If Dorothy's son Leonard and his friends got to the water first, it was theirs for the day. If the white kids got there first, the black kids found something else to do. If they arrived at the same time, they shared the pool, watching each other carefully and sometimes speaking as they swam and played.

Money was tight. Dorothy made clothes for herself and the children. She wore her shoes until her toes pushed through the leather. She sometimes went for a walk after putting the children's dinner on the table. Her dinner was the food that they left.

Langley didn't want to lose skilled computers like Dorothy. She had now been there for three years. Her work had no mistakes. She was always on time and always calm. She now looked after eight computers during her eight-hour work day. In 1946, Langley asked her to stay.

The Head of West Computing had always been a white woman. In April 1949 the position was empty, and Dorothy became Acting Head until Langley found someone else for the job. There were no black managers at the NACA, and certainly not any black women managers. She was clearly the only person for the job, but Langley was worried about upsetting white people in the town. They waited two years, and then they quietly made Dorothy Head of West Computing.

BREAKING THE SOUND BARRIER

Now the war was over, the engineers turned their attention to a new enemy – the sound barrier.

The latest wind tunnels at Langley could make winds at the speed of sound. The speed of sound is 1,225 kilometres per hour at sea level in dry air at 15°C – also called Mach 1. As a plane reaches Mach 1, air molecules in front of the flying plane build up, forming a shock wave. The shock wave makes a bang like a gun firing.

In October 1947, pilot Chuck Yeager prepared to break the sound barrier in the Mojave Desert. Some scientists were afraid that his plane would blow up and that Yeager would die. Neither thing happened. Yeager travelled faster than the speed of sound for the first time and it was a big step forward in the science of flight.

After Mach 1 was achieved, the NACA's next job was supersonic flight and then, hypersonic flight. In 1950, the NACA showed the world a new hypersonic wind tunnel. It could make wind speeds of Mach 7. The world of science fiction was becoming real.

What do these words mean? You can use a dictionary.
sound barrier   sea level   molecule   shock wave

CHAPTER 5
Becoming an engineer

In April 1951, Mary Jackson arrived at Langley. She was 26. Mary hadn't come far. She was from Hampton and she had grown up seeing the changes that the NACA was bringing to the area. Mary's high school results were excellent, and she went on to Hampton Institute, a black college. Most of Hampton's female students took their degrees in nursing or homemaking, but Mary chose maths and physics. She dreamed of becoming an engineer.

In 1942 she began her first job as a maths teacher away from home. Her father fell ill, however, and she had to return to care for him, finding a new job as secretary of the local USO*. The club was a centre for the city's black community, and Mary was at the heart of everything. She helped to find homes for military families, played the piano at social events, arranged dances and introduced newcomers to Hampton life. At all times she followed her family's belief in caring and sharing.

The USO centre was a great place for romantic wartime meetings too, and in 1944 Mary married Levi Jackson from Alabama. Mary refused to wear an all-white floor-length dress for her wedding. Instead she wore a short white dress with black gloves and shoes and a red rose.

The USO centre closed after the war, and Mary had a son, Levi Jr. Her husband worked at Langley Field as a painter while Mary looked after her son and filled her day with community activities. All her life, Mary loved the Girl Scouts**, and she led the local group. Many of

* Founded in 1941, the USO gives help to military members and their families.

** The Girl Scouts are a worldwide group for teenage girls to learn skills outside school.

her girls came from poor families. As well as helping with their maths homework and clothes making, she wanted to show them what was possible in the world. She took them on walks through the local parks, on visits to the factories where their parents worked and to the large home of the president of the Hampton Institute. There they saw a rich black family living in a beautiful house, just like in the movies.

In 1951, war broke out in Korea. The Russians were on the side of the North and the Americans fought with the South. America's super plane, the B-29 Superfortress, came under attack from the Russian MiG-15 fighter plane. The MiG-15 flew over Korean skies too fast to be seen, leaving the B-29 behind. It was a victory for the Russians in the military race. When reports came in from their spies, the US realised that the Russians were employing three times as many people in aeronautics and military factories.

Soviet MiG-15 plane

In April 1951, a husband and wife, the Rosenbergs, were in a New York court. Lawyers said they were

Russian spies, and their faces were on every newspaper in the US. The Cold War wasn't just happening in the skies above Korea or over in Europe, it was happening at home. Government films told Americans to look out for 'Reds' everywhere – at home, at work, at school – anyone could be a Communist spy. 'Watch out for Reds under the beds!' shouted the newspapers.

Were there spies at Langley? Some people believed the Russian MiGs used NACA designs. If you worked at Langley, the FBI* might turn up on your doorstep with questions at any time of day or night.

Many countries in Asia and Africa had been under European rule before World War II. As these countries won independence, the US wanted to keep them out of Soviet hands. These countries were starting to ask questions about segregation in the US and it was becoming very difficult for the US to explain. Black Americans were refused entry to restaurants every day of the week, but visitors from abroad were not used to it. They sent their stories home where they often made front page news. When Mahatma Gandhi's doctor was turned away from a restaurant because of his dark skin, the newspapers back in India were full of it. Why would these countries want to tie their future to America?

When Mary Jackson decided to return to full-time work, Langley was once again looking for good mathematicians and a long list of new jobs appeared in *Air Scoop*. Mary reported for work to Dorothy Vaughan on 15th April 1951 and she fitted right in.

One morning in 1953, Dorothy sent Mary over to a job on the East Side, working next to several white computers. Halfway through the morning, Mary needed the toilet.

* The FBI (Federal Bureau of Investigation) are America's homeland police.

The nearest toilets had no sign, which meant they were only for white women.

'Could you tell me where the toilet is?' Mary asked a white computer. The white girl looked at her friends and they laughed rudely.

'Why would we know where the Coloured toilet is?' she said.

Mary left the office angrily. There was segregation at Langley, she knew that. It was everywhere. But she had as much schooling as the white girls – if not more.

Later that day, still angry, she met Kaz Czarnecki on her way back to the West Area. Kaz had worked at Langley since 1939, after getting a degree in aeronautics from Alabama University.

'How's things?' asked Kaz.

Black women usually hid their anger from white men. They put on a face to protect themselves and their jobs. But Mary couldn't hold back. She told Kaz all about the women on the East Side.

Kaz listened. 'Why don't you come and work with the engineers?' he said.

It was a step on the road to Mary's dream of becoming an engineer herself.

Kaz immediately asked Mary to join his group, which ran a supersonic wind tunnel, and suggested that she take the Langley engineer training programme. The problem was, the classes took place at the whites-only Hampton High School. Mary could get a job as a cleaner at the High School, but she couldn't go through the door as an engineering student. Mary asked the school if she could join the classes. At first they said no. But she kept asking, and, in the end, she won. She began her course in the spring of 1956.

HAMPTON, VIRGINIA

The first slaves from Africa arrived in America in 1619, stepping off an English boat at Hampton, Virginia.

In the American Civil War, Hampton once again held an important place in black history. The American Civil War was fought from 1861 to 1865 and was the war to end slavery. It was fought between the Union (the North) and the Confederates (the South), and more Americans died in this war than in any other. President Abraham Lincoln and the North (the Yankees) won the Civil War and slavery in all the United States became against the law.

During the Civil War, a group of slaves escaped to Fort Monroe, on the Virginia coast, held by Union soldiers. The Confederate soldiers started a terrible fire in 1862 that destroyed the old city of Hampton. The slaves became free men in 1865, and built the new city of Hampton.

For a few years, the black community of Hampton, known for its bright young people, successful businesses and clever politicians, hoped for a brighter future. But then came the Jim Crow laws in Virginia, putting out the fire of hope for black equality.

CHAPTER 6

'Let's do it!'

As soon as Katherine Coleman could talk, her parents realised that she had a great way with people and a head for maths, just like her father. She counted everything she saw from leaves to steps to the stars at night. She threw question after question at her teachers and was moved up three years in class where she helped older students with their maths.

As a teenager, Katherine took a job every summer in the hotel where her father worked. She spent her lunchtimes in the hotel kitchen, practising her French with the cook. When she returned to school in the autumn, her perfect Parisian French amazed her teachers.

When Katherine was just fourteen, she finished high school and started at West Virginia state college for black students. She worked quickly through every maths course offered at the college. Her professor introduced her to very difficult maths ideas. In 1939, after finishing college, she accepted a job as a maths teacher.

The new job meant moving home. Katherine took the bus to her new job in Marion, Virginia. When the bus crossed the state line into Virginia, the driver stopped.

'All you black folks,' he called, 'you gotta go behind the Coloured line and sit in the back.' When they reached the black part of town, the bus driver told everyone to get off.

'I don't drive into the black area,' he said. 'Take a taxi from here.'

'Welcome to Virginia,' thought Katherine.

At the school in Marion, Katherine earned just $50 a month, even worse than the $65 paid to white teachers.

Katherine was poorly paid, but she was rich in love. In Marion, Katherine met Jimmy Goble, who was home on a break from college. They fell in love and got married in secret as married women were not allowed to be teachers.

Katherine always told people she was from West Virginia, a very different place from Virginia. There were hills where she came from and it was cool in the evening. During the Civil War, West Virginia had joined the Union, on the opposite side from Virginia. There was segregation in West Virginia, but it was much worse in Virginia.

In 1940 West Virginia decided to integrate students in their universities. Three black students were invited to be the first to study for higher degrees at West Virginia University. Katherine was one.

In the 1940 summer term, Katherine joined two other black students, and all three walked into the university on the first day. Katherine was intelligent, hardworking and calm. Most of the white students welcomed her, some were even friendly. The teachers treated her fairly, and the work came easily to her.

She stayed on the course for only the summer term, however. At the end of the first term, she found she was expecting her first child. She stayed at home for the next four years, in love with her husband, Jimmy, and happy with her three daughters, before returning to work as a teacher.

In August 1952 Katherine and Jimmy were in Marion for Jimmy's sister's wedding. Their three girls, now eleven, ten and nine, danced with their cousins while Katherine and Jimmy talked to Margaret, another of Jimmy's sisters, and her husband, Eric. They had come up from Newport News, where Eric ran the Newsome Park Community Centre.

'Why don't you come back with us?' said Eric. 'I can get Jimmy a job on the ships. In fact, I can get both of you jobs. There are jobs for black women at Hampton. They want mathematicians.' Eric knew everything that was going on in Hampton Roads. He knew many of the women at West Computing, including Dorothy Vaughan.

Katherine felt a fire growing inside her. She taught maths all day long, but at high school level. She knew she could do so much more. But did they want to move their three growing daughters from their quiet, safe life? Hampton Roads was far from their grandparents. It was hot. It was big.

'Let's do it!' said Katherine.

In one busy year, the Gobles fitted smoothly in. Eric found Jimmy a job as a ship painter, which paid the family bills. The girls loved living in such a large and exciting black community. After just two weeks in West Computing, it was clear to everyone that Katherine was the best mathematician they had ever seen. She was chosen to join the Flight Research Division (FRD). The job was at the heart of one of the most important and powerful groups at Langley.

Collecting her lunch box and handbag, Katherine walked over to her new office. Inside, the air was full of coffee and cigarette smoke. There were twenty desks, arranged like a classroom. Only one was free. Most of the people in the room were men, with a few white women. At the front sat Henry Pearson, the boss of FRD. Katherine sat at the empty desk, giving the man at the next desk her warmest smile. The man looked at her without speaking, then got up and walked away.

It was a test for Katherine. Had he walked out because she was black, or because she was a woman? Katherine pushed away her fears, ate her lunch at her new desk and remembered how lucky she was. Maybe he had walked out because it was lunchtime. Katherine had a warm personality and after the man discovered that, like him, Katherine was from West Virginia, the two became great friends.

CHAPTER 7
An uncertain future

Six months after the FRD borrowed Katherine Goble from West Computing, Dorothy Vaughan asked for a meeting with Katherine's boss, Henry Pearson.

'Either give her more money or send her back to me,' said Dorothy.

Henry was not a fan of women in the workplace, but as soon as Katherine had begun work, the whole department knew that she was one of their best. Henry did what Dorothy asked. A white computer in Katherine's department had already asked Henry for more money, but he had refused.

'I'm sure you'd like to give her more money too,' said Dorothy. Henry had no choice.

The FRD engineers were free-thinking and very bright. Katherine was not scared of them. She was confident in her own maths, she wanted to know everything, and she questioned the engineers all day long. They spent their lives thinking about flight, and they were never too bored or too busy to discuss it.

The skies were becoming more and more crowded with aircraft, and safety was a growing problem. A small plane had fallen out of the sky and crashed. Katherine's first job was to work out why. She spent months checking the maths to understand the final movements of the plane. She discovered that a much larger plane had passed through the same place half an hour before, leaving a path of rough air behind it. When the small plane crossed through the larger plane's path, the pilot lost control. Nobody knew until then that it took so long for the air to return to normal. Katherine's work led to changes in air traffic rules. From now on, the time and space between flight paths was carefully calculated.

From the very beginning, Katherine felt completely at home at Langley. She couldn't believe that someone was paying her to do maths, the thing that came most naturally to her in the world. She loved the work and the community. The toilets in her department had no signs. She avoided the segregated cafeteria by eating her lunch at her desk. She always remembered her father's words to her, 'You are no better than anyone else, and no one is better than you.'

Jimmy Goble had high hopes for his family and wanted to move them to a better area. He and Katherine chose a house in a middle-class part of town. It was a perfect plan, until Jimmy started to have headaches and became seriously ill. It took the doctors months to find the problem.

A year later in 1956, just before Christmas, Jimmy died. The community took care of Katherine and her girls in their days of sadness.

Katherine had promised Jimmy she would keep their bright, happy daughters on the path to a good future. On the first day of the new term, just two weeks after Jimmy died, the girls were back at school.

Katherine spoke to their head teacher. 'Don't be kind to them,' Katherine said. 'Nothing special. They're going to college, and they'll need to be strong and brave. They have to learn.'

At home, she gave them new rules. 'You will have my clothes ready in the morning,' she said. 'And dinner when I come home.'

Katherine knew she must not fall to pieces. At just thirty-eight years old, she was alone with three children. Her children were not her only worry, however. The Langley computers were facing an uncertain future. In the mid-1950s the first electronic computers arrived. The engineers thought they were awesome. They used them to make calculations for a 'rocket plane', a new kind of vehicle that could fly high enough and fast enough to get into space.

Early electronic computers could only do one job at a time. They were the size of a small room. They cost a million dollars and they made mistakes. But Dorothy Vaughan looked at the IBM* machines and realised that they were the future. She was the first to sign up for Langley's computer programming course, and she suggested that the other West Area computers do the same. Dorothy was never one to look back.

* Started in 1911 in the US, the IBM company made early computers.

CHAPTER 8
Sputnik

There were two big news stories at the beginning of October 1957. Neither story showed the US in a good light.

Soldiers help Little Rock Nine into school

The first blow came from Little Rock, Arkansas. Nine black teenage schoolchildren were trying to enter Little Rock's all-white Central High School. They were testing a new law that said US public schools could not be segregated. However, the state governor did not believe in integration. He called out his National Guard to lock the school doors. President Eisenhower was angry and sent in US soldiers to take the nine young people into school. Photos went around the world. The black students held tight to their books, soldiers all around them, while an angry white crowd screamed and threw bottles at them. It was ugly.

Soviet satellite shoots across US

Across America, people were looking up at the night sky from their gardens and the street. 'Can it see us?' they wondered. 'Can it drop bombs on us?' Katherine and her team stood outside and watched too. An object like a moving star passed overhead.

The 'moving star' was Sputnik 1, the world's first satellite. When Radio Moscow announced its launch, President Eisenhower tried to pretend it was nothing.

'It's a small ball in the air,' he said.

But the American people disagreed. 'It's a technological Pearl Harbor,' they said. The Soviets were first into space. The space race had begun.

Sputnik 1 flew over the US every 98 minutes. Radio Moscow read out a list of the American cities it would fly over. A few days later, they added a new location to the list: Little Rock, Arkansas. It was two-zero to the Soviets.

The skies were already full of NACA successes. There were passenger planes, bombers, transport planes and fighter aircraft. Research into space travel, however, had been slow. When President Eisenhower announced his government's programme, the Soviets were already putting Sputnik 2, carrying space dog Laika, and Sputnik 3 into space.

'This is not science fiction,' said President Eisenhower. Ordinary Americans were not so sure. It would cost billions of dollars and what good was it? Four reasons were given: to be ready for any attack, to show the world the achievements of the US, to learn about outer space and most importantly, to go where no one had been before. Eisenhower promised that Americans would see their countrymen in outer space as soon as possible.

President Eisenhower had answers for why and when, but not how. Meeting after meeting was held at Langley. The top engineers had worked for years in aeronautics and many of them were secret lovers of science fiction. This was their chance to discuss orbits, rockets and the physics of space. Katherine's boss, Henry Pearson, arranged some space technology talks. Each engineer was given a different subject to present to the group. Katherine prepared the calculations. When the engineers gave her instructions, she listened closely and asked questions. She wanted to understand how things worked. She was right there, learning with the engineers. They were writing the textbook of space in real time.

Katherine knew the real action was taking place in the meetings and talks, behind closed doors.

'Why can't I go to the meetings?' she asked the

engineers. They always told her the results afterwards. Why not just be there?

'Girls don't go to the meetings,' said the engineers.

'Is there a law against it?' she asked.

'It's not personal,' they said. 'It's just the way we do things. It's always been like that.'

Men were engineers and women were computers. Men did the thinking; women did the calculations. Men gave the orders; women took the notes. But Katherine wanted more than that. Katherine showed every day that women were equal to men, and she was probably the best mathematician in the room.

'Why can't I go to the meetings?' she asked again.

'OK,' they said finally. 'You can go!' Now Katherine was part of the space programme.

ORBITING THE EARTH

Any spacecraft has first to travel through the earth's atmosphere. It has to break through the sound barrier, reaching Mach 18, then escape the pull of the earth's gravity and lock smoothly into the 29,000 kilometres per hour speed needed for orbiting the earth. On the return trip, the vehicle has to push through the thick atmosphere, causing extremely high temperatures to build outside the spacecraft.

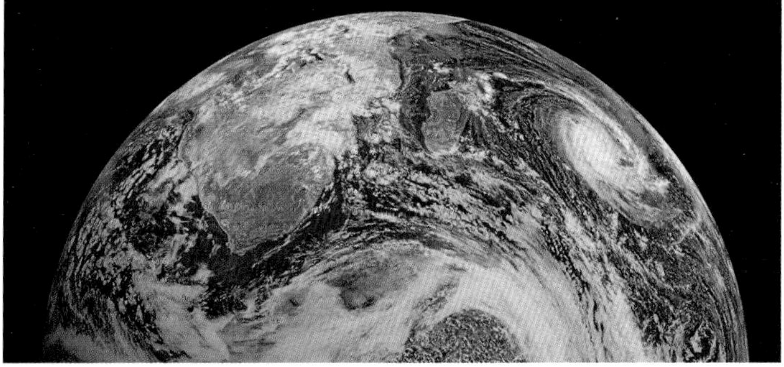

There had been almost no need for general computers in the different parts of the NACA since the arrival of the IBM machines. Each office had its own mathematicians, who worked full-time as part of the team. A note went around the NACA in May 1958. 'From this date,' it said, 'the West Area Computers Unit is closed.' It was a sad day for Dorothy Vaughan. She had become the first black manager in the NACA's history, but now she was just one of the girls again.

In October 1958, the US government decided to bring all its space operations into one centre at the NACA. The NACA had been quiet and little known. The new centre – called NASA* – would be world famous.

The NASA scientists and engineers were no longer NACA nuts. Now they were the leaders of the space age. Katherine's office, the FRD, became the Space Task Group (STG). A group of forty-five people, they gave the country's first manned space programme a plan and a name. The plan: to orbit the earth, to find out if humans could live in space and to bring the man and spacecraft back safely. The name: Project Mercury.

Back on the ground, the US Civil Rights movement was growing. Fifteen-year-old Claudette Colvin and forty-two-year-old Rosa Parks were taken to prison in Montgomery because they refused to give their bus seats to white passengers. Black people in Montgomery stopped using the buses, which travelled around the city empty and losing money. Again, it was world news. The leader of the Montgomery bus action was a young preacher called Martin Luther King.

Virginia was proud of its space programme. But it hung onto segregation, even though it was against government law. In autumn 1958, Virginia's new governor locked

* National Aeronautics and Space Administration

the doors of any school that tried to integrate black and white pupils. Thirteen thousand white and black pupils in three cities were locked out of school. Most of the schools reopened in 1959, and began moving slowly towards integration. In one area of Virginia, however, the segregationists refused to change, continuing to lock children out of school for five years. They could send a man into space, but they couldn't put black and white children into the same classroom.

CHAPTER 9
Project Mercury

Katherine was now a forty-year-old single mother. She loved to follow her college basketball team, she never missed Sundays at church and she and her friend Eunice went to singing practice once a week. One Sunday in 1958, a handsome soldier appeared at church. Jim Johnson had fought in the Korean War, and now worked in Hampton as a postman.

'Ladies, he's single,' said the preacher.

Jim and Katherine began going out together almost immediately. Jim understood that work was a big part of Katherine's life. He knew what she had already achieved as a black woman. And he understood her long hours at Langley. After the war, the NACA had been an 8 to 4.30 kind of place. Now, with the space race on, leaving the building by 10 pm was a good day.

Seven astronauts were chosen for Project Mercury, and were given a NASA office next door to the Space Task Group at Langley. They trained hard and had classroom instruction in engineering and space science. The Mercury Seven were as famous as film stars.

The first flight of Project Mercury would be suborbital – an astronaut would travel into space and come straight back down. The astronaut was Alan Shepard and he called his capsule Freedom 7. Katherine's group of engineers were calculating the exact path of Freedom 7 from launch to landing in the Atlantic Ocean. The capsule needed to land close to waiting ships so that Shepard could be quickly pulled to safety. The maths had to be perfect.

'Let me do it,' said Katherine. 'Tell me where you want the man to land, and I'll tell you where to send him up.'

FREEDOM 7

THE CAPSULE

NASA tests showed that a long thin capsule with a pointed nose would not push away the heat of re-entry. A short fat capsule with a rounded nose would be better. The Freedom 7 capsule was approximately 1.9 metres wide and 2 metres high – just large enough for one astronaut.

Mercury capsule shape A

THE FLIGHT PATH

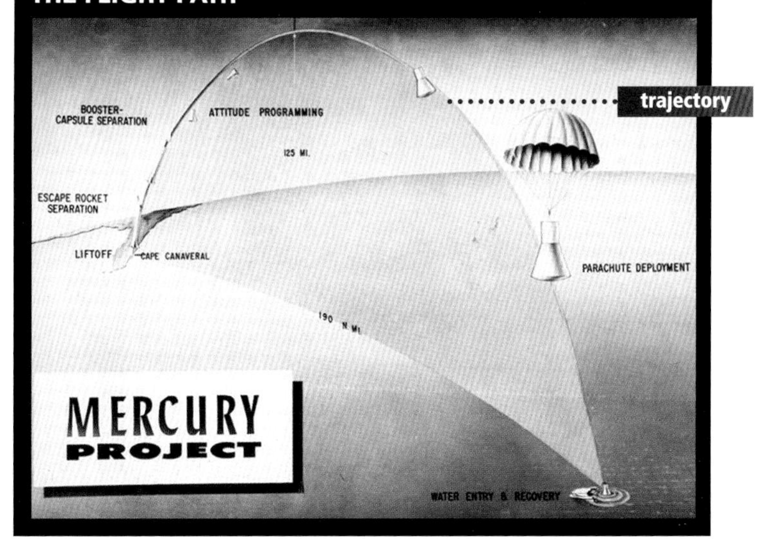

trajectory

To work out the trajectory, Katherine had to think about the earth's gravity, the fact that the earth is not perfectly round and the speed at which the earth turns. She worked it all out, and put it into a report in October 1959. Her report went through ten months of meetings, changes and checks before it came out in September 1960. During those long busy months and pages of numbers, Katherine and Jim Johnson decided to get married. She signed her first report as Katherine Johnson, the name that history remembers.

In 1960 Langley proudly showed off its new electronic computers. All the engineering groups sent their calculations to the machines now. Young male scientists were attracted to them, so that computing, once a female job, was becoming a job for men.

Dorothy Vaughan was fifty, and she looked to the future, not the past. She trained again, learning how to program. Her job now was to turn the engineer's calculation questions into the computer language FORTRAN.

In February 1961 a new President walked into the White House. President John F. Kennedy immediately introduced a new law. The government must act to ensure equality for all workers, of every race, religion, colour or nationality. It was a step forward for black civil rights.

Then on 12th April 1961, another first for Russia. Cosmonaut* Yuri Gagarin became the first person in space and the first person to orbit the earth.

'Why weren't we first?' asked the Project Mercury director. 'We were so close!' NASA was not happy to be second again, but they kept their attention on their mission.

Less than a month later, on 5th May 1961, NASA was ready. Live on television, in front of 45 million

* Russian astronauts are called *cosmonauts*.

Americans, US astronaut Alan Shepard went into space for the first time. The flight lasted just 15 minutes and 22 seconds, went 187.5 kilometres above earth, covered 487.3 kilometres and was nowhere near Gagarin's achievement.

President Kennedy was confident about his team at NASA, however. 'I believe we should go to the moon!' he said. Kennedy wanted to land a man on the moon and return him safely to earth in the next ten years. Kennedy's goal surprised everyone at NASA. They hadn't even put a man in orbit yet!

Good news for the space teams, however, led to some difficult changes. NASA had grown too big for its Langley home, and had to move. Powerful Texans in the government wanted the space centre in Texas, and Houston won the day. The Langley employees had to decide. Should they stay in their lovely home by the sea, with its warm winters and delicious seafood? Or should they move to be with the work that they lived for?

Katherine was asked to move to Houston, but her husband, Jim, wanted to stay near their families. She turned down the offer. Langley wasn't closing, and there was still work on Project Mercury. Electronic computers were the future even for Katherine. Before that, however, she had an important job on her desk. It was Katherine against the electronic computer.

CHAPTER 10

'Get the girl to check the numbers!'

Sending a man into space was hard enough. Getting him back home safely kept the space team awake at night. The Mercury capsule was ready to go. But NASA refused to launch before they were 100 percent sure of a successful mission. Every part had been tested and tested again. Everything depended on getting the physics and the maths right. Just one number in the wrong place and the mission could end in disaster.

Nobody understood this better than astronaut John Glenn. He was the guy going up in the tin can. He ran miles every day. He practised getting out of the capsule in the Back River behind Langley over and over again. He went through hundreds of possible situations where every part of the capsule failed.

In August 1961 a second Russian cosmonaut orbited the earth seventeen times, spending nearly a full day in space. The press were impatient. 'Hurry up!' they shouted, as the January 1962 launch was moved to February because of bad weather. John Glenn stayed calm. He spoke optimistically to the press, and he kept in perfect shape.

The date was set: 20th February 1962. John Glenn wanted the numbers checked one final time. The IBM computer had produced the orbital path. But Glenn had been a pilot in the Korean War, and pilots didn't like computers. He wanted total control over his spacecraft. Every engineer and mathematician had double-checked the computer's numbers, and found a mistake at least once. And what if the computer lost power during the flight?

Now a computer like Katherine was different. She could look at figures and say, 'That doesn't look right'. And she could answer questions. John Glenn believed in his engineers. And his engineers believed in their mathematician.

'Get the girl to check the numbers!' said Glenn. 'If she says the numbers are good, then I'm ready to go.'

For a day and a half, Katherine worked through every minute of Glenn's flight. At the end of the job, every number in the papers on her desk matched every number from the electronic computer. John Glenn was ready to go.

FRIENDSHIP 7: COMMUNICATIONS

In order to keep communication with the orbiting spacecraft at all times, Langley set up the Mercury tracking network. This was a line of eighteen communications stations equally spaced around the earth and some in the oceans on ships. Powerful satellite receivers picked up the radio of the Mercury spacecraft as it passed overhead. The information from the receivers was used to check and change the flight path in real time. Red lights came on if there was any trouble.

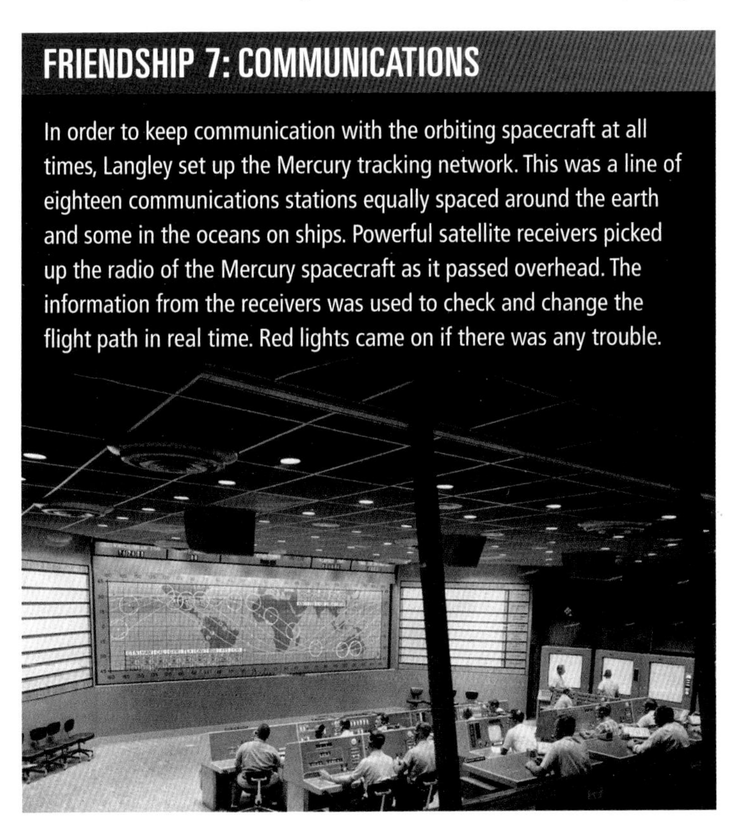

THE MERCURY PROJECT

20th February, 1962 At dawn, the skies were clear. Around 135 million people were watching their televisions. Katherine was in her office.

At 9:47 am the Atlas rocket sent Friendship 7 into perfect orbit.

Mission Control in Houston, Texas, cleared Glenn for seven orbits.

During Orbit 1 the capsule began to pull backwards and forwards. Glenn took control of the capsule as if it was a plane.

At the end of Orbit 2 a switch showed that the heat shield could be loose. The shield would protect Glenn from extremely high temperatures as the capsule re-entered the atmosphere.

At 4 hours, 33 minutes into the flight, the rockets fired. The capsule prepared for re-entry, with Glenn and Mission Control fearing the worst. Mission Control lost radio communications with Glenn. There was silence. Katherine closed her eyes tight.

14 minutes later Glenn's voice suddenly reappeared, sounding happy and calm. He continued his return, landing in the sea just 64 kilometres from the waiting boats.

21 minutes after landing, the US Navy lifted Glenn out of the water.

Time in orbit 4 hours, 48 minutes, 27 seconds.

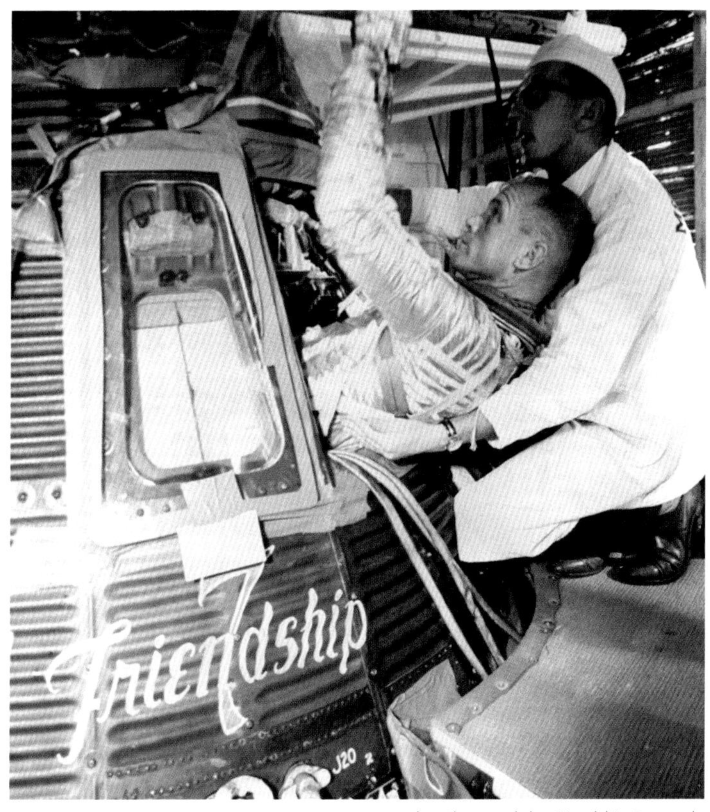

John Glenn and the Friendship 7 capsule

The mission was successful. John Glenn was the first American in orbit and became an American superstar. He met the President and appeared on the front pages of newspapers around the world. The black community celebrated Katherine's part in the mission, and her photograph appeared too, on the front pages of black newspapers like the *Pittsburgh Courier*.

'I'm just doing my job,' said Katherine, and then she turned her attention to the next job: the Apollo space programme and landing on the moon.

CHAPTER 11
Man on the moon

In August 1963, came a huge moment in the fight for civil rights. Three hundred thousand people, led by Martin Luther King, joined the March on Washington. Bob Dylan and Mahalia Jackson sang in front of the Lincoln Memorial.

Then, Dr King stood up to speak. He had written some notes, but he pushed them away. 'I have a dream,' he began. Martin Luther King had one message for the United States: the dream of black people and the American dream were one and the same.

In the early 1960s, of all the black employees at Langley, only five were engineers and only sixteen had the job title mathematician. Langley needed more engineers, and this time they sent teams out to the black colleges in the Southern states. Greater numbers of black scientists began to arrive, many taken under the wing of Mary Jackson, NASA's and America's first female African-American aeronautical engineer.

Mary helped everyone. She brought students from Hampton's public schools to Langley for tours, to see the engineers at work and to meet an astronaut if they were lucky. She invited a white female engineer to give a joint lecture with her to an all-black group of high school girls. The girls saw it was possible for an exciting workplace to include a woman who looked like them. Mary found places for new members of the team to live. She and Levi invited them to their house for dinner, a place to go if they missed home. In 1979, Mary was made Langley's Women's Program Manager, where she fought for the working rights of women of all colours.

James T. Kirk (left), Spock, and Uhura

In 1966, a new science fiction show appeared on American TV and quickly became popular. It was called *Star Trek*. The Starship *Enterprise* set off from the earth to explore deep space, with an international team of different races and colours, led by Captain James T. Kirk. They left from a United Earth, where war was in the past. And there on the ship's bridge was Lieutenant Uhura, a black female Communications Officer.

After the first season, the actor who played Uhura, Nichelle Nichols, said she wanted to leave the show. The next weekend she was at a civil rights meeting, and was introduced to 'her greatest fan'. It was Martin Luther King. King was a 'Trekkie', and it was the only TV show he allowed his children to watch. The show put black people at the controls.

The actor told King her plans to leave. 'No!' he said. 'You can't leave the show. When we see you, we see ourselves, and we see ourselves as intelligent and beautiful and proud. You have a special part that brings to life what we are fighting for – equality.' After the meeting, Nichelle decided to stay in the show.

A great sadness hit the space programme in February 1967 when Apollo 1 was ready for a test launch at Cape Canaveral in Florida. Three astronauts were inside. A sudden electrical fire destroyed the rocket in seconds, killing all three astronauts. NASA was shaken to its heart. The men weren't thousands of miles away in space, they were on the ground. The road to the stars was hard.

There was more heartbreak for the world in 1968, especially the black community, when Martin Luther King was shot dead.

It would cost the US $24 billion to win the space race and many Americans were not sure that it was worth it. For many black people, the space race had little to do with their everyday lives. A popular song from Gil Scott-Heron, 'Whitey* on the moon', played on black radio stations.

The engineers at NASA changed the design of the Apollo spacecraft, and checked everything again and again over the next nine Apollo missions. And then came Apollo 11.

The Apollo 11 spacecraft was designed to carry three astronauts. The plan was for two astronauts – Neil Armstrong and Buzz Aldrin – to land on the moon, while a third astronaut, Michael Collins, circled the moon in the command module.

If the path of the command module was wrong when the astronauts piloted their lander back up from the moon, Katherine knew the two vehicles would not meet. The command module was the astronauts' bus back to earth. If they missed it, they would die in space. 'It must be less dangerous than a Sunday ride in the car,' thought Katherine as she worked out orbits around the moon. Katherine was at Langley sixteen hours a day, going home

* 'Whitey' is a (usually racist) word for a white person.

to check on her daughters in the late afternoon. This last step – the dance between the moon, the lander and the waiting command module – was the most difficult.

On 16th July 1969, it was very hot in Hampton. Too hot to think, to sleep, to do anything. Katherine had given her best. But was it good enough? Katherine was among the 200,000 NASA employees and the 650 million people around the world who were watching Cape Canaveral on their TV screens. At 9.37 a Saturn V rocket launched the Apollo 11 spacecraft with its three astronauts on their way to history.

Four days after launch, the lander, called the Eagle, left the Apollo command module. Astronaut Neil Armstrong thought they had a fifty-fifty chance of landing on the moon the first time. But Katherine thought differently. She was confident in her numbers.

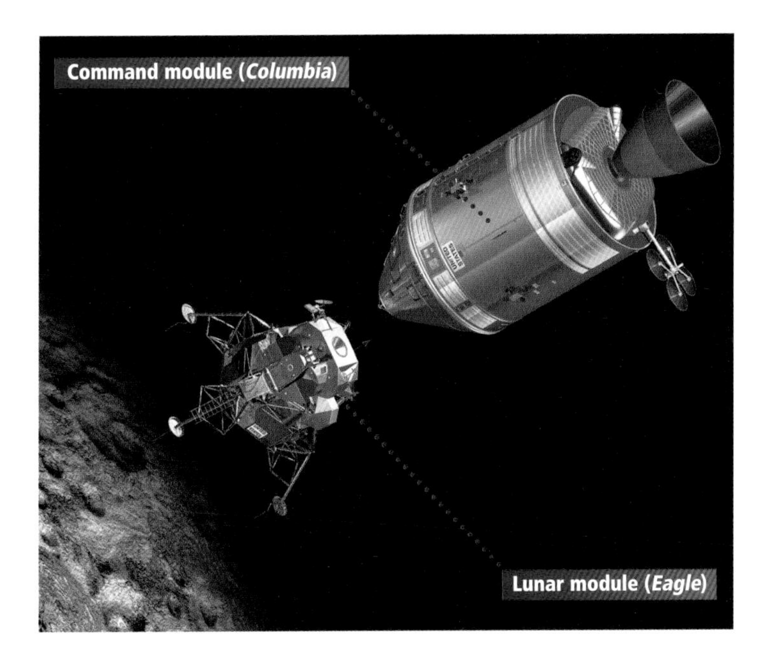

APOLLO 11 MOON MISSION

1,533,792 KILOMETRES

8 DAYS, 3 HOURS, 18 MINUTES, 35 SECONDS IN SPACE

21 HOURS, 36 MINUTES ON THE MOON'S SURFACE

650 MILLION PEOPLE WATCHED ON TV

Buzz Aldrin and the Eagle on the moon's surface

The Eagle landed on the moon at 20.17 on 20th July 1969. The landing was perfect. The world watched and waited for the door of the Eagle to open. But it wasn't until the early hours of the next morning that Neil Armstrong stepped onto the moon.

The rest of the mission was also a success. The command module orbited the moon every ninety minutes. Armstrong and Aldrin successfully piloted their lander back to the mother ship. They travelled back through space for three days, passing through the earth's atmosphere and into the ocean below.

As Katherine waited for the safe rescue of the Apollo 11 astronauts from the Pacific Ocean, she was already thinking about Mars. And then, why not Jupiter and Saturn? Katherine knew that once you took the first step, anything was possible.

THE RACE

Apollo 11 took just over four days to land on the moon. A mission to Mars could take between six and nine months. However, scientists around the world are working on ways to land humans on Mars.

CLIMATE CHANGE

Mars has a very thin atmosphere that is 96 percent carbon dioxide. The planet is dry and cold, and has dangerous dust storms, which may last for months.

The climate on Mars used to be wetter and warmer with a thicker atmosphere. There are mountains and valleys and scientists believe there was water in the past. There may still be water below the surface.

Why did the climate of Mars change? Was there ever life on Mars? Could humans live on Mars? Scientists at NASA have many questions. And they are not the only ones. India, China, Japan, the United Arab Emirates, Russia and Europe all have Mars space programmes.

LIFE ON MARS

What would it be like to live on Mars? You would probably never come back to earth because a return journey would use too much fuel. Communications with earth would be slow and you'd live in a small community. If you were outside, you'd have to wear a spacesuit all the time. But scientists are working out how to grow plants on Mars, so you wouldn't go without fruit and vegetables. And you'd be one of the first space explorers!

DID YOU KNOW?

Mars is called the Red Planet because there is lots of iron in the ground. When iron mixes with air, it turns red.

TO MARS

Mars Rover

★ Would you like to move to Mars? Why? / Why not? ★

You can see Mars in the night sky from where you live. It looks redder than the other stars in the sky.

THE RED PLANET: IN NUMBERS

- It's **half** the size of earth and **twice** the size of our moon.
- It has **two** moons called Phobos and Deimos.
- It takes longer to orbit the sun than earth, and one Mars year lasts **687** earth days.
- The surface gravity on Mars is less than on earth. **100 kilos** on earth weighs only **38 kilos** on Mars.
- The hottest it gets on Mars is **30°C.** The coldest temperature is **–140°C.** The coldest it gets on earth is **–89°C.**

What do these words mean? You can use a dictionary.

climate carbon dioxide dust surface fuel planet iron

Chapters 1–3

Before you read

You can use your dictionary.

1 Look at New Words on page 64. Match a word with each sentence.
Someone who:
   a) has no control over their own life.
   b) flies into space.
   c) goes to war.
   d) designs bridges and aeroplanes.
   e) leads a church community.

2 Choose the correct adjectives.
   a) By law, men and women, black and white, young and old are all **equal / fair**.
   b) He fought in two wars – he was a **company / military** man all his life.
   c) The **powerful / romantic** storm destroyed a large area of forest.
   d) Students from **integrated / segregated** schools understand different beliefs and cultures better.

3 Complete the sentences using these words.
bombs calculations control degree missions physics victory
   a) After her ... in the 100 metre race, she went out with her friends to celebrate.
   b) If you want to be an engineer, I think you should study ... .
   c) My cousin wants to study for a ... in politics at university.
   d) A number of countries have ... to send astronauts to the moon again.
   e) The government tried to ... the information that reached the people, but it failed.
   f) Thousands of ... were dropped on London in World War II.
   g) A computer can do ... millions of times faster than a person.

4 The word 'figure' has two meanings. What are they? Why is this reader called *Hidden Figures*, do you think?

After you read

5 Answer these questions.

a) Why was Dorothy washing socks when she was a maths teacher with a college degree?

b) What change in employment law made life better for African-Americans in 1941?

c) How had the war changed the Hampton Roads area of Virginia?

d) Why were black people in America angry about President Roosevelt's call to free the Jews in Nazi Germany?

e) Why did Miriam Mann's husband think she was going to lose her job?

f) What did the NACA use its wind tunnels for?

Chapters 4–6

Before you read

6 Answer these questions.

a) What makes up the earth's atmosphere?

b) Why do you weigh more on earth than on the moon?

7 What do you think?

World War II lasted five years. How would you feel when you heard the news that the war was over? What would you do?

After you read

8 Are these sentences true or false?

a) Dorothy didn't need to be careful with money after the war.

b) The sound barrier was broken for the first time in the Mojave Desert in 1947.

c) Hopes for black equality after the American Civil War did not last long in Virginia.

d) The Russian MiG-15 wasn't as fast as the American B-29.

e) Mary was not able to study engineering at Hampton High School.

f) Segregation was worse in Virginia than in West Virginia.

- **g)** Katherine left her degree programme at West Virginia University because of how she was treated.
- **h)** It took a long time for the NACA to realise that Katherine Goble was an excellent mathematician.

9 What do you think?
The next chapter is called 'An uncertain future'. What could this chapter be about?

Chapters 7–9

Before you read

You can use your dictionary.

10 Answer these questions.

- **a)** If you **launch** a rocket, are you sending it into space or bringing it home?
- **b)** If you are the **communications** officer on a spaceship, what is your job?
- **c)** What is a **satellite** used for?
- **d)** If an astronaut **orbits** the earth twice, how many times will they see their own country?

11 What do you think?
What event started the space race?

After you read

12 Answer these questions.

- **a)** Who were the Little Rock Nine, and what were they trying to do?
- **b)** 'It's a small ball in the air,' said President Eisenhower in 1957. What was he talking about?
- **c)** Who travelled in Sputnik 2?
- **d)** What is the biggest problem for a spacecraft on its return to earth?
- **e)** What was Project Mercury?
- **f)** Who were the Mercury Seven?
- **g)** Who was the first man in space?

13 Correct the information in these sentences.

- **a)** Dorothy told Henry Pearson that Katherine could not work for him any more.
- **b)** Dorothy did not think that the IBM computers would be successful.
- **c)** Katherine was invited to join the space meetings.
- **d)** Dorothy left NASA when the West Area Computers Unit closed.
- **e)** Dorothy was not interested in learning how to use the new computers.

14 What do you think?
Imagine you are helping to choose America's first astronauts. What kind of person will you look for? Write a list.

Chapters 10–11

Before you read

15 What do you think?
How did Katherine feel when Yuri Gagarin orbited the earth?

After you read

16 Put these events in the right order.

- **a)** John Glenn orbits the earth three times.
- **b)** John Glenn asks Katherine to check the numbers for his space flight.
- **c)** Martin Luther King is shot dead.
- **d)** Neil Armstrong steps on the moon.
- **e)** *Star Trek* is first shown on American TV.
- **f)** Three astronauts die as their rocket is about to launch.
- **g)** Three hundred thousand people go to Washington and call for equal rights for black and white Americans.
- **h)** Mary Jackson was made Women's Program Manager.
- **i)** Katherine married Jim Johnson.

17 What do you think?

- **a)** Is it right for a government to spend a lot of money on space programmes instead of on problems at home?
- **b)** Should governments be sending missions to Mars? Why / Why not?

NEW WORDS

What do these words mean?

astronaut (n) ....
atmosphere (n) ....
bomb (n & v) ....
calculate (v) .... / calculation (n) ....
communications (n) ....
community (n) ....
control (n & v) ....
degree (n) ....
disaster (n) ....
engineer (n) ....
equal (adj) .... / equality (n) ....
figure (n) ....
gravity (n) ....
integrate (v) .... / integration (n) ....
launch (n & v) ....
military (adj) ....
mission (n) ....
orbit (n & v) ....
physics (n) ....
power (n) .... / powerful (adj) ....
preach (v) .... / preacher (n) ....
research (n) ....
rocket (n) ....
satellite (n) ....
science fiction (n) ....
segregate (v) .... / segregation (n) ....
slave (n) .... / slavery (n) ....
soldier (n) ....
tunnel (n) ....
victory (n) ....